THE WESTERN STATES

by Sarah Glasscock

Table of Contents

Introduction... 2

Chapter 1 Geography and Climate.................... 4

Chapter 2 People and Industry........................ 12

Chapter 3 Places to Visit in the Western States..... 20

Conclusion... 28

Solve This Answers....................................... 30

Glossary.. 31

Index.. 32

Introduction

The United States has many **regions**. A region is a large area made up of places that share some features. Two features are geography and climate. Another feature is **industry** (IHN-duhs-tree). An industry is a group of businesses that produce and sell similar products or services.

California, Hawaii, Montana, Nevada, Utah, and Wyoming make up a region called the West. Long ago, dinosaurs roamed this region. A huge sea covered part of the land, too. Now you can see dinosaur bones that were dug up in Montana. You can float in the Great Salt Lake, which is a part of that old sea.

▲ These people are digging for dinosaur bones on the prairie.

This book will tell you about the western states. You'll learn about the region's geography and climate, and find out why people moved to the region. You'll also learn about the work people in the West did in the past, and the work people do today. Finally, you'll tour some fun places in the western states.

▲ Six states make up the region known as the West.

Chapter 1

Geography and Climate

In this chapter, you'll find out about the geography and climate of the western states. You'll learn about streams, rivers, and lakes. You'll also learn about the mountains and **deserts** found in the region.

Land: Mountains

Tall mountains rise in each of the western states. In fact, some of the tallest mountains in the United States are in this region. They are joined in **mountain ranges**. A mountain range is a group of mountains.

▲ Mount Whitney is the highest peak in the Sierra Nevada. It is 14,494 feet (4,418 meters) high.

The Sierra Nevada (see-YAIR-uh nuh-VAH-duh) lies in California and Nevada. This mountain range is about 400 miles (644 kilometers) long. Many people heading west in wagons had to cross the Sierra Nevada. They went though **passes** in the mountains. A pass is a low place in a mountain range.

The Pacific Coast Ranges are also in this region. A section of these mountains runs along the Pacific Ocean in California. The mountains stop the flow of wet air from the ocean. The wet air falls as rain in the area between the Pacific Ocean and the range. As a result, there is more rain there than in other parts of California.

The Rocky Mountains go through the western states of Utah, Montana, and Wyoming. The Continental Divide follows the tops of the Rocky Mountains. It is also called the Great Divide. Rivers that are east of the Continental Divide flow into the Atlantic Ocean or the Gulf of Mexico. Rivers that are west of the Continental Divide flow into the Pacific Ocean.

#1 Solve This

You can hike along the 3,100-mile (4,988-kilometer) trail that follows the Continental Divide. The trail is usually open only during July, August, and September. If you wanted to hike the entire trail from July to September, about how far would you need to travel each day?

Math ✓ Point

How did you get the information to solve this problem?

CHAPTER 1

Deserts

A desert is a place that gets less than 10 inches (25 centimeters) of rain or snow in a year. North America has four main deserts. Three of them are in the western states. A desert is either a cold desert or a hot desert.

▲ This map shows the western deserts.

The Great Basin Desert is a cold desert. Snow falls there. The Great Basin has an area of 190,000 square miles (492,100 square kilometers). Few cactuses grow there, but low bushes, such as sagebrush, are able to grow there.

The Sonoran (suh-NOR-uhn) Desert is the hottest desert in North America. It has been as hot as 117°F (47°C). The Sonoran Desert has an area of 120,000 square miles (310,800 square kilometers). Huge saguaro (suh-WAHR-oh) cactuses grow there.

#2 Solve This

California is 163,707 squares miles (424,000 square kilometers) in area. Nevada has an area of 110,567 square miles (286,367 square kilometers). The area of Utah is 84,904 square miles (219,900 square kilometers).
In which state or states would the Sonoran Desert fit?

Math ✓ Point

Is your answer reasonable? Explain why or why not.

GEOGRAPHY AND CLIMATE

The Mojave (moh-HAH-vee) Desert is also a hot desert. It is smaller than the other deserts in North America, and it is the driest. Most places receive less than 6 inches (15 centimeters) of rain a year. Bushes and cactuses still grow in the Mojave Desert, though.

The Kau (KOW) Desert is in Hawaii. It is called a desert, but it is not a true desert. About 30 inches (76 centimeters) of rain fall there every year. Still, the land is dry like a desert, and it is often hot. Very few plants can grow there. This makes it like a desert.

✓ **Point**

Make Connections
How is the desert in this photograph like other deserts you have seen or read about? How is it different?

▲ the Mojave desert

CHAPTER 1

Water: Streams and Rivers

The western states have many streams, rivers, and lakes. In the mountains, melting snow runs into streams. The streams flow into rivers or lakes. The rivers join other rivers, or they flow to the ocean.

Some of the water from rivers and lakes is used for electric power and **irrigation** (eer-ih-GAY-shuhn). Because very little rain falls in the western states, farmers have to water their crops with water from rivers and lakes. Towns and cities use this water, too. The water is used for drinking, bathing, and washing clothes and dishes.

▲ Many different kinds of salmon can be found in California, including steelhead, coho, and sockeye salmon.

GEOGRAPHY AND CLIMATE

A Great Lake

The Great Salt Lake really is salty. It's so salty that fish can't live in the water. If you jump into the lake, you'll bob right to the surface. The high amount of salt in the water makes you float.

Why is the lake so salty? A huge freshwater lake called Lake Bonneville once covered areas of Utah. **Evaporation** (ih-VA-puh-RAY-shuhn) caused Lake Bonneville to dry up. The Great Salt Lake is a part of that ancient lake. It is salty because it has no outlet to the sea. The salt in the water has nowhere else to go. The rivers that flow into the Great Salt Lake dump even more salt into the water.

Historical Perspective
Glen Canyon Dam

In the 1930s, dams were built across many rivers. Those projects gave jobs to hundreds of workers. The dams produce power. They also help stop floods. But today we know that damming rivers has hurt the habitats, or living places, of animals and plants. Because of the dams, beautiful places like Glen Canyon are now under water.

CHAPTER 1

Climate: Rain and Snow

Mountains are important to the climate of the western states. For instance, the mountain ranges in California keep rain from falling in the deserts. When air hits the mountains, it rises. As the air rises, it cools. This causes rain to fall on one side of the mountains. Then the air drops to the other side of the mountains. It gets warm and dries out. As the air drops, it creates a **rain shadow**. The land under a rain shadow receives little rain, and there are few clouds.

It's a Fact
One winter, the temperature in Havre (HAH-vuhr), Montana, rose 43°F (6°C) in fifteen minutes. Warm winds called Chinook winds blew in over the Rocky Mountains. The winds only hit the area east of the Rocky Mountains. *Chinook* is a Native American word that means "snow eater."

▲ Snow falls in every western state—including Hawaii!

GEOGRAPHY AND CLIMATE

Temperature

You've shivered in the mountains. You've sweated in the deserts. So you know that the temperatures in this region can be very different.

In January, the temperature in Las Vegas, Nevada, is about 60°F (15°C). You can drive to the Spring Mountains in about thirty minutes. If you go, take a sled. You will find snow on the ground. The Spring Mountains are about 30°F (1°C) cooler than Las Vegas.

Half Moon Bay is on the California coast. In July, it's about 65°F (18°C). If you drive 50 miles (80 kilometers) west to Tracy, it will be about 95°F (35°C).

#3 Solve This

If the temperature in Half Moon Bay is 45°F (7°C) in December, what do you predict the temperature in Tracy will be?

Math ✓ Point
What steps did you take to solve the problem?

▲ Half Moon Bay, California

Chapter 2

People and Industry

I n the past, people came to the West to search for gold and silver. They also moved to the region to ranch and farm. Today, people move there because of the climate, the beauty of the land, and for work.

Becoming States

The western states are some of our newest states. Before they were states, they were **territories** (TAIR-ih-tor-ees). A territory is an area of land that is ruled by a country. The United States owned the territories. One by one, they became states.

#4 Solve This

In what year will Montana celebrate its 150th year as a state?

STATE	DATE ADMITTED	NUMBER
California	September 9, 1850	31st
Nevada	October 31, 1854	36th
Montana	November 8, 1889	41st
Wyoming	July 10, 1890	44th
Utah	January 4, 1896	45th
Hawaii	August 21, 1959	50th

Hawaii Becomes a State

Hawaii is about 2,400 miles (3,860 kilometers) from the mainland United States. It has had a different history from other states. As the time line below shows, Hawaii was once ruled by kings and a queen.

A.D.	
300–700	First settlers arrive from Polynesia (pah-luh-NEE-zyuh), islands to the west of Hawaii.
1778	English Captain James Cook arrives.
1778–1820	New settlers begin to arrive.
1795	Kamehameha (kuh-may-uh-MAY-uh) I becomes king.
1819	Kamehameha II becomes king.
1824	Kamehameha III becomes king.
1854	Kamehameha IV becomes king.
1863	Kamehameha V becomes king.
1872	Lunalilo (loo-nah-LEE-loh) becomes king.
1891	Liliuokalani (lee-lee-uh-oo-kuh-LAH-nee) becomes queen.
1893	Liliuokalani is overthrown.
1898	Hawaii is annexed by the United States. When a place is annexed, it is joined with another country.
1900	Hawaii becomes an American territory.
1959	Hawaii becomes the fiftieth state.

◀ Queen Liliuokalani

CHAPTER 2

Mining Yesterday

In 1848, James Marshall was building a sawmill. He found a lump of gold. Then he found more and more gold. His boss, John Sutter, wasn't happy about the gold. He wanted his sawmill finished. If people heard about the gold, Sutter knew they would come to his land to search for it. He tried to keep the gold a secret, but word spread. Soon, thousands of people from the United States and all over the world rushed to California to look for gold. The Gold Rush was on!

Eyewitness Account

James Marshall tells about finding gold:
"I reached my hands down and picked it up; it made my heart thump, for I was certain it was gold. The piece was about half the size and shape of a pea. Then I saw another."

James S. Brown tells about seeing James Marshall's gold:
"I picked the largest piece [of gold], worth about fifty cents, and tested it with my teeth, and as it did not give, I held it aloft [up] and exclaimed, 'Gold, boys, gold!'"

▲ Men hoping to strike it rich mined for gold.

PEOPLE AND INDUSTRY

Mining Today

Mining is still an important industry in many of the western states. Today, gold, silver, coal, oil, and natural gas are mined in the region.

Montana is nicknamed the Treasure State because of the coal, oil, metals, and natural gas that can be mined there. Nevada is sometimes called the Mining State. More gold is produced there than in any other state. Wyoming leads the United States in production of coal. The largest coal mine in the nation is near the town of Wright, Wyoming.

✔ Point

Think About It
What is the main idea of this page? What details support the main idea?

▲ Trains carry coal from Wyoming to other states in cars called hoppers. A coal train has 100 hoppers. Each hopper is filled with about 100 tons of coal.

CHAPTER 2

Ranching and Farming Yesterday

Even before the Gold Rush, settlers were moving west to start ranches and farms. The East was getting crowded. There was still plenty of open land in the West. Ranchers could let their cattle or sheep graze as much as they wanted.

Groups of settlers in wagon trains followed trails to the West. The Mormons, a religious group, made their own trail from Kansas to what is now Utah. They felt they would have more freedom to practice their religion in the West.

It's a Fact
The invention of barbed wire made it easier and cheaper for farmers to fence in their land. Fences kept roaming cattle and sheep out of crops. But fences blocked the way of large cattle drives from Texas. And Native Americans weren't able to look for food and water on land they had always lived on.

▲ Some Mormons pushed or pulled handcarts across the country instead of riding in wagons. Carts didn't cost as much as wagons did.

PEOPLE AND INDUSTRY

Ranching and Farming Today

Livestock—cattle, sheep, hogs, and turkeys—is raised in every state in the West. The animals graze on grasses, but ranchers and farmers also grow hay and grain to feed them. The next time you eat a turkey sandwich, think about California. More turkeys are raised there than in any other state.

Farmers in Hawaii grow pineapples, sugarcane, coffee, and flowers. Many fruits, vegetables, and nuts are grown in California.

They Made a Difference

Alice Waters owns a restaurant in Berkeley, California, that serves fruits and vegetables grown by local farmers. She also started a program that helps students plant gardens at their schools. The students prepare and serve the food from their gardens in their cafeterias.

▲ California is famous for its wines. The grapes used to make the wines grow on vines.

The Movies

Many movies, TV shows, and cartoons are made in Los Angeles, California. The city is the center of the film industry. Los Angeles has sunny days and mild weather. So people are able to shoot movies and TV shows outside all year long.

Did you know that some of the *Star Wars* movies were filmed in Death Valley, California? Did you know that Kanab, Utah, is known as Little Hollywood? More than 100 westerns have been filmed in Kanab.

▲ The film industry is located in Hollywood, a part of Los Angeles.

Careers

Animators draw the cartoons you watch in movies and on television. They draw the cartoons by hand or on a computer. Then each drawing is filmed to show movement. It takes twenty-four to thirty pictures to create one second of film. Animators also create special effects, such as spaceships and dinosaurs.

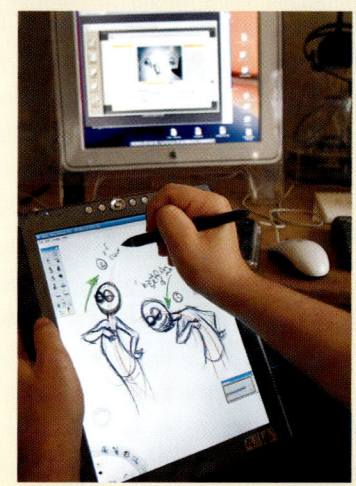

PEOPLE AND INDUSTRY

Tourism

Many tourists visit the western states each year. They spend money on hotels, meals, and gas. They pay fees to go to parks and to ski in the mountains. Because of this, **tourism** is one of the main industries in the region. Tourism is the business of providing services to tourists.

What do you like to do on vacation? Hunt for dinosaurs? Go to a rodeo? Look for gold? In the next chapter, you'll read about some of the fun places in the western states where you can do all those things.

It's a Fact
Las Vegas, Nevada, has more hotel rooms than any other city in the world. There are almost 150,000 hotel rooms in the city.

▲ The Going-to-the-Sun Road crosses the Continental Divide. Some people call it a "don't look down drive" because the road is so steep.

Chapter 3

Places to Visit in the
Western States

Are you ready to take a tour of some fun places in the western states? You'll see skeletons of dinosaurs. You'll visit national parks, and cities and towns. You'll swim with brightly colored fish. You might even find gold!

Long ago, dinosaurs roamed parts of Montana. Many of their bones have been found there. To learn more about these huge creatures, take a trip down the Montana Dinosaur Trail. You can stop at museums and parks. You can watch people as they search for more bones. You might even see some ancient dinosaur eggs.

Cheyenne Frontier Days, Wyoming

The world's largest rodeo is held every summer in Cheyenne, Wyoming. It's part of Cheyenne Frontier Days. For ten days, there are parades, musical acts, rides, and a pancake breakfast. You can visit Native American storytellers, dancers, and drummers.

At the rodeo, you can take a "behind the chutes" tour. Chutes are the narrow tunnels that bulls and horses are led through before they are released into the ring. Of course, there aren't any animals in the chutes during the tour, so it's safe for you to walk through the chutes and even into the ring!

▲ People of all ages take part in the Cheyenne rodeo.

CHAPTER 3

Bryce Canyon National Park, Utah

Wind and water have worn away rock in Bryce Canyon National Park. They've carved shapes called **hoodoos** from the rock. Long ago, people thought hoodoos were people or animals frozen in stone.

The hoodoos are tall and thin. Some are as tall as a ten-story building. Hoodoos have bands of color. The color comes from minerals in the rock. The best place to view the hoodoos is from the bottom of Bryce Canyon. You can hike to the bottom or ride a horse there.

▲ Two to four feet of hoodoo rock can wear away every 100 years.

PLACES TO VISIT IN THE WESTERN STATES

Virginia City, Nevada

Would you like to visit the "richest place on Earth"? That's what Virginia City was once called. Two men found gold nearby in 1859. Their find, called the Comstock Lode, produced billions of dollars in gold and silver.

Virginia City grew from a mining camp filled with tents into a busy city. About 20,000 people lived there. But they began to find less and less gold and silver. Many moved away. Today, only about 1,500 people live in Virginia City.

Primary Source

Writer Mark Twain lived in Virginia City in the 1860s. He was a miner for a while. Twain wrote this about Virginia City:

"The city and all the great mountainside were riddled [filled] with mining shafts. There were more mines than miners … To make money, and make it fast, was as easy as it was to eat your dinner."

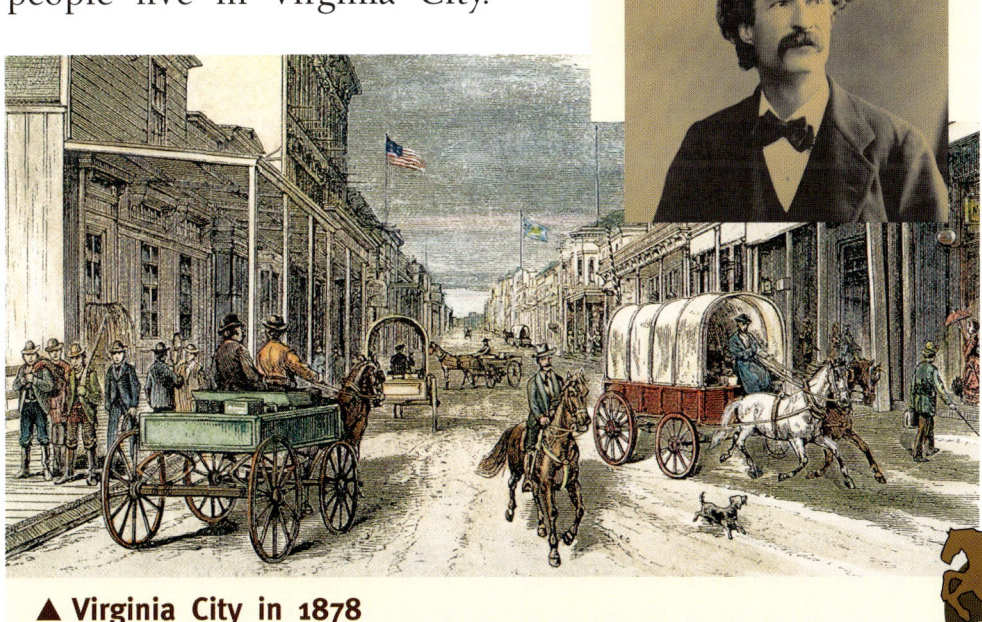

▲ Virginia City in 1878

23

CHAPTER 3

San Francisco, California

The city of San Francisco is surrounded on three sides by a **bay** and the Pacific Ocean. A bay is part of an ocean that cuts into the coast. San Francisco has cool summers and mild winters. In the morning, you might see fog.

The Golden Gate Bridge is about 1.7 miles (2.7 kilometers) long. If you walk across the bridge, wear a coat. It can be very windy.

On Saturdays, people shop in food markets on Stockton Street in Chinatown. Many Chinese people moved to San Francisco during the Gold Rush.

This man is painting the Golden Gate Bridge a color called International Orange.

PLACES TO VISIT IN THE WESTERN STATES

Sequoia National Park, California

When you visit Sequoia (sih-KWOY-uh) National Park, you will see the largest trees in the world. These giant trees are sequoias. The only place they grow naturally is on the west side of the Sierra Nevada. The sequoias are very old trees. They are between 1,800 and 2,700 years old.

The table below gives the height of the five tallest trees.

THE TALLEST SEQUOIAS

Tree	Height
General Sherman	274.9 feet (83.8 meters)
General Grant	268.1 feet (81.7 meters)
Lincoln	255.8 feet (78.9 meters)
Washington	254.7 feet (77.6 meters)
President	240.9 feet (73.4 meters)

▲ "General Sherman" is taller than a 27-story building. It's as wide as a three-lane highway.

CHAPTER 3

Death Valley National Park

Death Valley is a desert basin. It stretches across eastern California and western Nevada. It includes the lowest point, 282 feet (86 meters) below sea level, in the Western Hemisphere.

Death Valley only receives about 2 inches (5.1 centimeters) of rain a year. The temperature reached 134°F (57°C) in Death Valley in 1913.

So why would you want to visit Death Valley? You wouldn't want to go there in the summer. But after the spring rains, Death Valley blooms with flowers.

Not all of Death Valley is flat. The table below shows the elevation of places in Death Valley. Elevation is how high above sea level a place is.

ELEVATIONS IN DEATH VALLEY

Place	Elevation
Telescope Peak	11,048 feet (3,367 meters)
Bald Peak	7,764 feet (2,366 meters)
Bullfrog Mountain	4,959 feet (1,511 meters)
Death Valley Buttes	3,017 feet (920 meters)

▲ Death Valley

PLACES TO VISIT IN THE WESTERN STATES

Hanauma Bay, Hawaii

Hanauma (hah-NOW-mah) Bay was named the most beautiful beach in the United States in 2004. It has white sand, and the water is deep blue. Colorful fish, eels, and sea turtles swim in the bay.

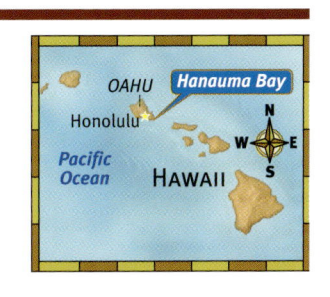

People used to throw bread, peas, and snacks to the fish. That wasn't good for them. By the 1980s, about 10,000 people visited the bay every day. It got too crowded. In 1990, the park cut the number of visitors to about 3,000 per day. No one is allowed to feed the fish.

#5 Solve This

Predict about how many people will visit Hanauma Bay this year. (The park is open every day of the year.)

Math ✓ Point

What steps did you follow to get your answer?

▼ Hanauma Bay is the crater of a volcano that filled with water.

27

Conclusion

Your tour of the western states has come to an end. You've read about the region's mountains and deserts, streams and rivers, and the Great Salt Lake. Were you surprised to find out that snow falls in the mountains of every state in the West?

The western states were some of the last territories to become part of the United States. People moved west to ranch and farm, but the discovery of gold and silver is what really started the rush to the area. Mining, ranching, and farming are still important industries in the West. Movies and tourism are also main industries.

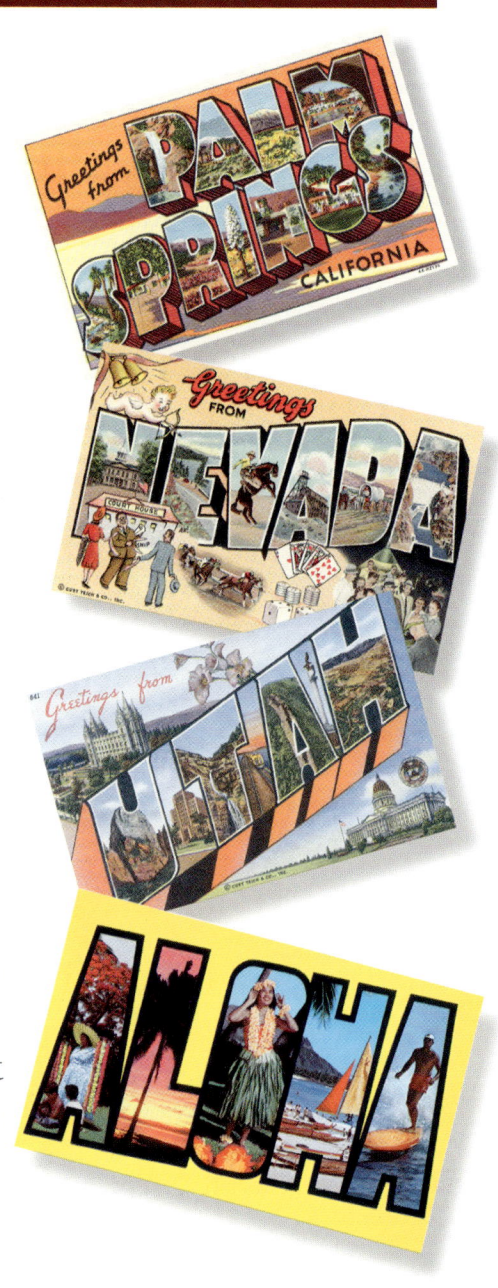

You discovered some of the fun places to visit in the western states. Cities and towns, sandy beaches and sand dunes, national parks—this region has it all.

What do you think will happen to the western states in the future? Will people from other areas still move there to build better lives? Will they still visit to see the natural beauty? How about you? Are your bags packed yet for a trip to the West?

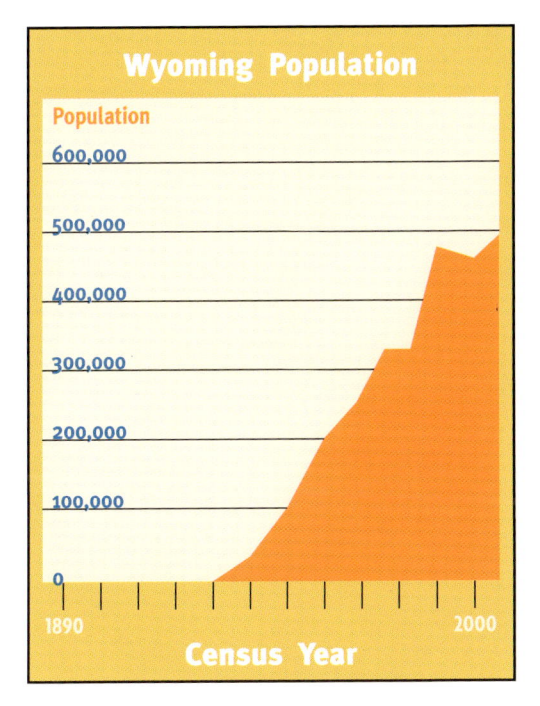

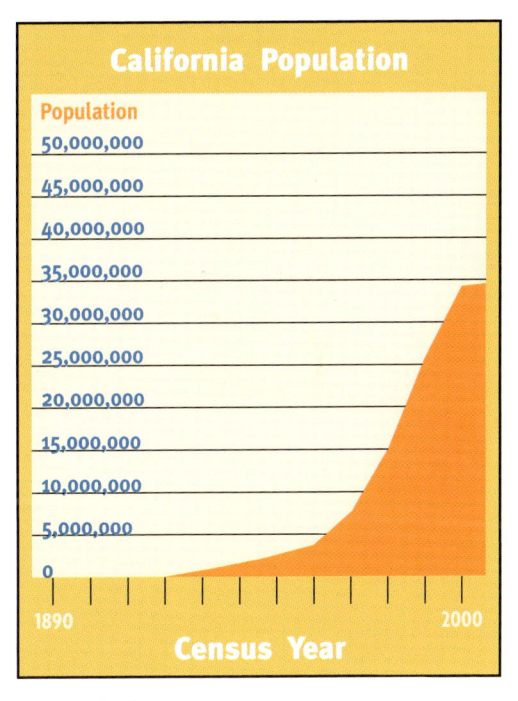

▲ Wyoming has the smallest population of the western states. California has the largest population. What do you think the population of each state will be in 2010?

Solve This Answers

1. Page 5

Add up the total number of days in July, August, and September.

31 + 31 + 30 = 92 days

Divide the length of the trail by the number of days.

3,100 miles (4,988 kilometers) / 92 = 33.7 miles (54.2 kilometers) per day.

2. Page 6

The area of the Sonoran Desert is 120,000 square miles (310,000 square kilometers). Only California, with an area of 163,707 square miles (424,000 square kilometers), is large enough to hold the entire desert.

3. Page 11

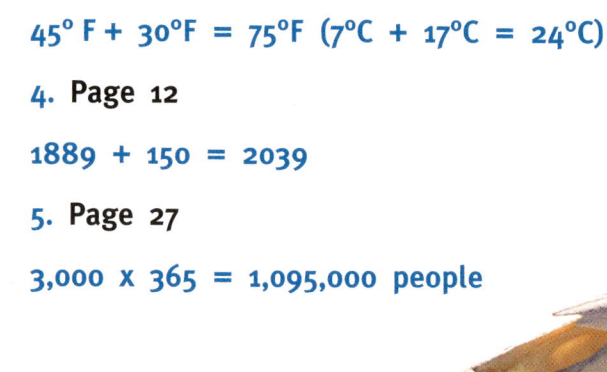

45° F + 30°F = 75°F (7°C + 17°C = 24°C)

4. Page 12

1889 + 150 = 2039

5. Page 27

3,000 x 365 = 1,095,000 people

Glossary

bay	(BAY) a part of an ocean that cuts into the coast and forms a hollow curve (page 24)
desert	(DEH-zuhrt) an area that receives less than 10 inches (25.4 centimeters) of rain a year (page 4)
evaporation	(ih-VA-puh-RAY-shuhn) the act of changing from a liquid into a gas (page 9)
hoodoo	(HOO-doo) a formation that is created when water and wind wear away rock (page 22)
industry	(IHN-duhs-tree) a group of businesses that produce and sell similar products or services (page 2)
irrigation	(eer-ih-GAY-shuhn) the practice of supplying land with water from streams, rivers, or lakes (page 8)
mountain range	(MOWN-tuhn RAYNJ) a group of mountains that are connected, such as the Rocky Mountains (page 4)
pass	(PASS) a low place in the mountains where people and animals can cross (page 5)
rain shadow	(RAYN SHA-doh) the area on one side of a mountain that gets much less rain than an area on the other side (page 10)
region	(REE-juhn) a large area made up of places that share some features, such as geography and climate (page 2)
territory	(TAIR-ih-tor-ee) an area of land that is controlled by a country (page 12)
tourism	(TOR-ih-zuhm) an industry that provides goods and services to people who travel for pleasure (page 19)

Index

bay, 11, 24, 27
Bryce Canyon National Park, 22
California, 2, 5, 10–11, 14, 17–18, 24–26
Cheyenne, 21
Continental Divide, 5
Death Valley, 18, 26
desert, 4, 6–7, 10–11, 26, 28
evaporation, 9
farming, 8, 12, 17, 28
Gold Rush, 14, 16
Great Basin Desert, 6
Great Salt Lake, 2, 9, 28
Half Moon Bay, 11
Hanauma Bay, 27
Hawaii, 2, 7, 17, 27
hoodoo, 22
industry, 2, 14–19
irrigation, 8
Kanab, 18
Kau Desert, 7
Las Vegas, 11
Los Angeles, 18
Marshall, James, 14
mining, 14–15, 23, 28
Mojave Desert, 7

Montana, 2, 5, 15, 20
Montana Dinosaur Trail, 20
Mormons, 16
mountain range, 4–5, 10
movie industry, 18, 28
Nevada, 2, 11, 15, 23, 26
Pacific Coast Ranges, 4
Pacific Ocean, 5, 24
pass, 5
rain shadow, 10
ranching, 12, 16–17, 28
region, 2–5, 11–12, 15, 19, 28–29
Rocky Mountains, 5
San Francisco, 24
Sequoia National Park, 25
Sierra Nevada, 5, 25
Sonoran Desert, 6
Spring Mountains, 11
Sutter, John, 14
territory, 12, 28
tourism, 19
Tracy, 11
Utah, 2, 5, 9, 16, 18, 22
Virginia City, 23
Wyoming, 2, 5, 15, 21